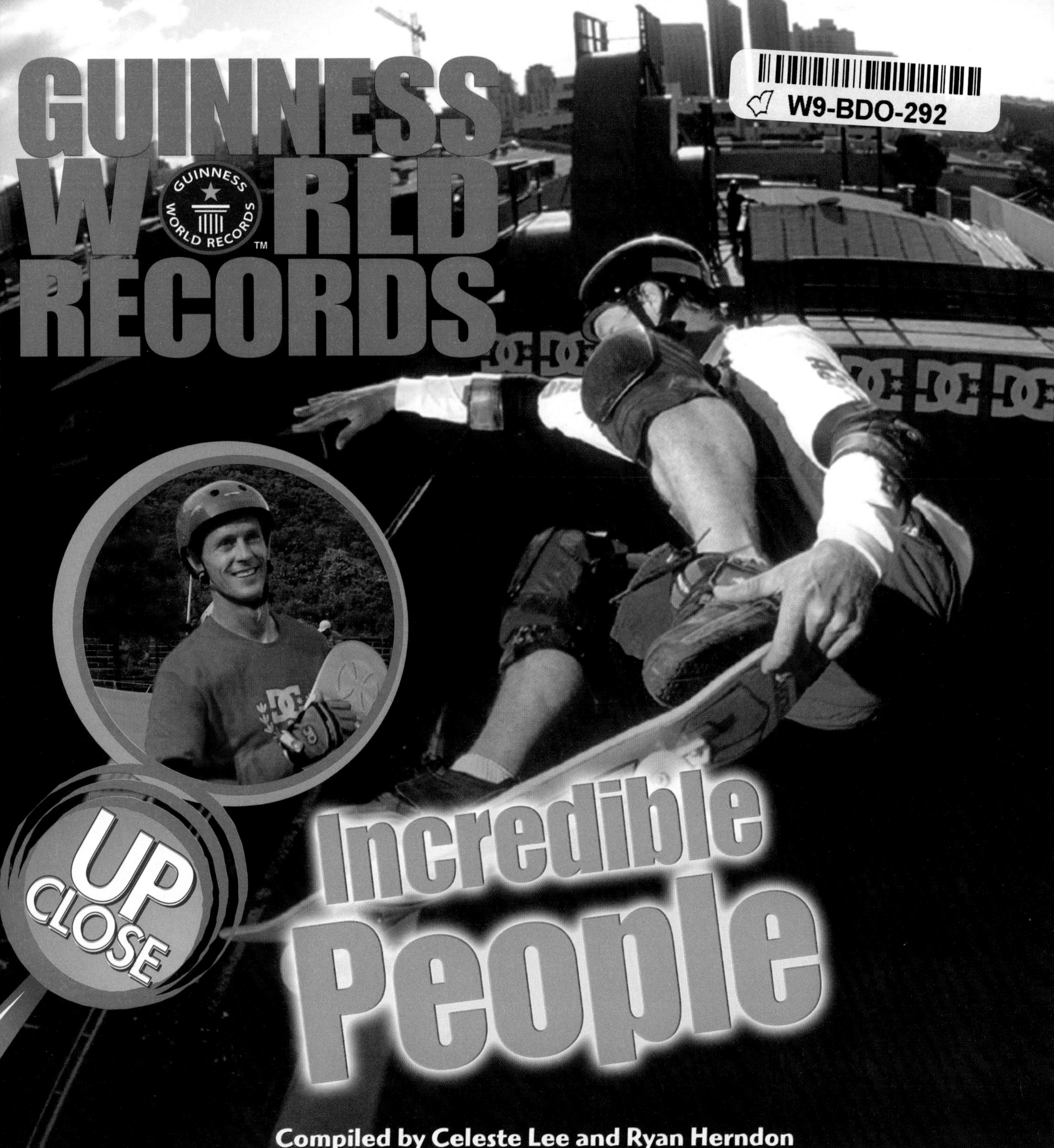

Compiled by Celeste Lee and Ryan Herndon

For Guinness World Records: Laura Barrett, Craig Glenday, Della Torra Howes, Stuart Claxton, Betty Halvagi

SCHOLASTIC INC.
New York Toronto London Auckland Sydney
Mexico City New Delhi Hong Kong Buenos Aires

Attempting to break records or set new records can be dangerous. Appropriate advice should be taken first, and all record attempts are undertaken entirely at the participant's risk. In no circumstances will Guinness World Records Limited or Scholastic Inc. have any liability for death or injury suffered in any record attempts. Guinness World Records Limited has complete discretion over whether or not to include any particular records in the annual *Guinness World Records* book.

Guinness World Records Limited has a very thorough accreditation system for records verification. However, while every effort is made to ensure accuracy, Guinness World Records Limited cannot be held responsible for any errors contained in this work. Feedback from our readers on any point of accuracy is always welcomed.

ISBN 0-439-79191-X

Designed by Michelle Martinez Design, Inc.
Photo Research by Els Rijper
Records from the Archives of Guinness World Records

12 11 10 9 8 7 6 5 4 3 2 1 6 7 8 9 10/0

Printed in the U.S.A.

First printing, January 2006

Visit Guinness World Records at www.guinnessworldrecords.com

ZOOM IN!

For over 50 years, Guinness World Records has documented the world's most amazing record-breakers in every field imaginable. Today, the records in their archives number more than 40,000.

In this collection, we'll zoom in on the lives of 25 incredible people who hold extraordinary records of achievement in history, sports, and the arts. We'll celebrate their excellence and explore the stories behind the records, from the fastest pumpkin carver to the youngest reigning monarch. Finally, we'll visit with five superstar record-holders who are the "Best of the Best!"

Go up close and get inspired — Guinness World Records style!

A Record-Breaking History

The idea for Guinness World Records grew out of a question. In 1951, Sir Hugh Beaver, the managing director of the Guinness Brewery, wanted to know which was the fastest game bird in Europe — the golden plover or the grouse? Some people argued that it was the grouse. Others claimed it was the plover. A book to settle the debate did not exist until Sir Hugh discovered the knowledgeable twin brothers Norris and Ross McWhirter, who lived in London.

Like their father and grandfather, the McWhirter twins loved information. They were kids just like you when they started clipping interesting facts from newspapers and memorizing important dates in world history. As well as learning the names of every river, mountain range, and nation's capital, they knew the record for pole squatting (196 days in 1954), which language had only one irregular verb (Turkish), and that the grouse — flying at a timed speed of 43.5 miles per hour — is faster than the golden plover at 40.4 miles per hour.

Norris and Ross served in the Royal Navy during World War II, graduated from college, and launched their own fact-finding business called McWhirter Twins, Ltd. They were the perfect people to compile the book of records that Sir Hugh Beaver searched for yet could not find.

The first edition of *The Guinness Book of Records* was published on August 27, 1955, and since then has been published in 37 languages and more than 100 countries. In 2000, the book title changed to *Guinness World Records* and has set an incredible record of its own: Excluding non-copyrighted books such as the Bible and the Koran, *Guinness World Records* is the best-selling book of all time!

Today, the official Keeper of the Records keeps a careful eye on each Guinness World Record, compiling and verifying the greatest the world has to offer — from the fastest and the tallest to the slowest and the smallest, with everything in between.

Peak Performances

Faster, higher, longer, better! Certain people are simply exceptional athletes. Some have trained since childhood, while others discovered their talents by chance. These shining stars hurdled all obstacles to cross the finish line as record-holders. We invite you to meet these peak performers, who dug in and found that something extra when it counted.

Outracing challengers is an ancient competition.

Fast and fearless Richard Petty, driver of legendary Car Number 43, reigns as "The King" of the National Association of Stock Car Auto Racing (NASCAR). His career (1958 – 1992) spans the sport's transformation from dirt tracks in North Carolina to giant domed speedways across America. He started his engine in a record-setting 1,184 races — the most starts for any NASCAR driver — and achieved an unrivaled 126 pole positions. A 7-time champion, he is tied with the late Dale Earnhardt, Sr., for Most NASCAR Titles.

RECORD 1

Most Wins in a NASCAR Season

During the superspeedy year of 1967, Petty won an astounding 27 NASCAR races, earning the **Most Wins in a NASCAR Season**. Petty had won 11 races by the series midpoint in July. He took 5 out of the next 8 races, leading into a breakneck winning streak of 10 races in a row! This streak set the mark for the most consecutive NASCAR wins ever, an achievement many racing buffs believe is unequaled. Although Cale Yarborough is the record-holder for **Most Consecutive NASCAR Championships**, Petty beat *him* in a photo finish at the "Firecracker 400" in 1984. When the flag came down, Petty had won his 200th NASCAR race.

The winner's circle is called Victory Lane.

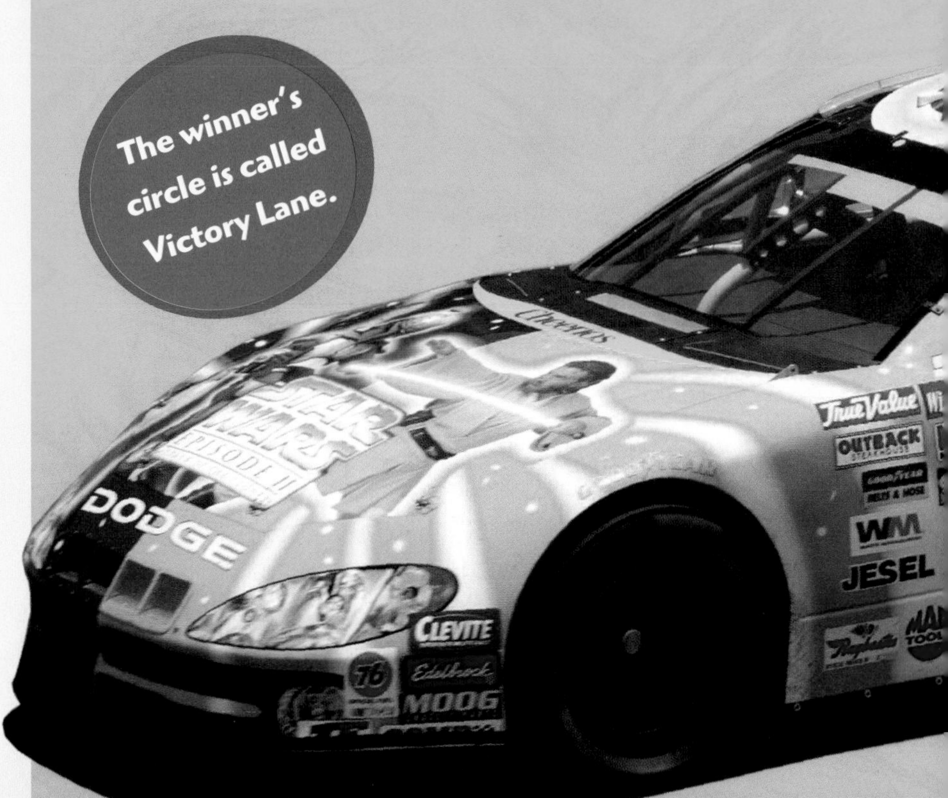

FACT:

In true stock car style, Richard Petty won 7 Daytonas in 4 different cars: a Plymouth, Dodge, Oldsmobile, and Buick.

MOWED DOWN

Turn a weekend chore into a suped-up sport! If you're 18 and have a rideable lawn mower, you can compete in the cutting-edge sport of lawn mower racing. Some categories allow for special mower modifications, but the actual lawn-cutting blades must be removed. The mowers race year round, revving up for the Challenge of Champions before a fresh season sprouts in September.

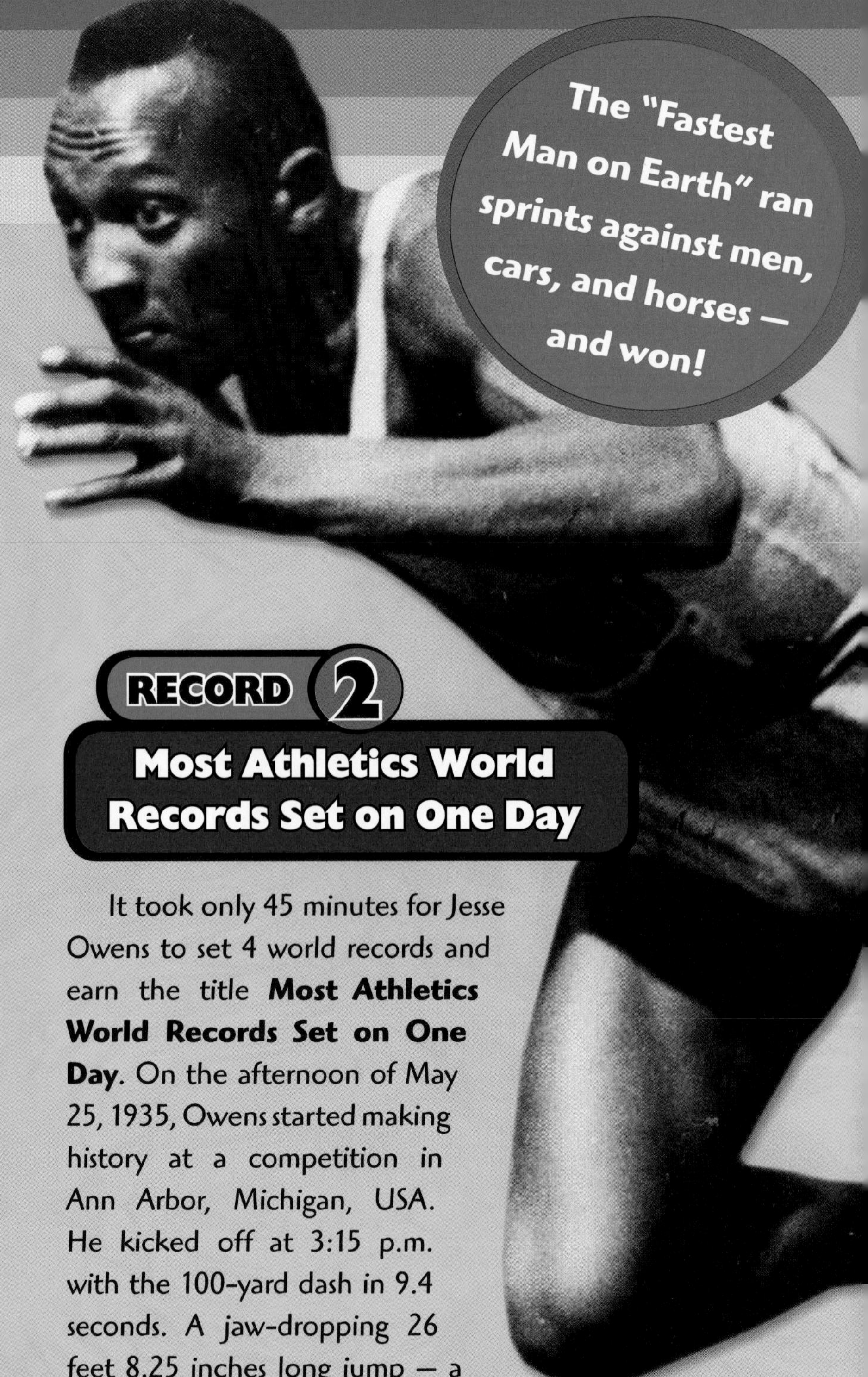

The "Fastest Man on Earth" ran sprints against men, cars, and horses — and won!

A determined athlete hurdles every obstacle — from pain to prejudice.

James Cleveland Owens was born on September 12, 1913, on a farm near Danville, Alabama. His parents were sharecroppers whose ancestors had been slaves. The family moved to Cleveland when James was 8. A schoolteacher couldn't understand his southern accent, so she called him "Jesse" instead of "J.C." Jesse Owens represented the USA at the Berlin Olympics of 1936, where he set new world records in running and long jump, and utterly defied Adolph Hitler's prejudices. Now people around the world knew his name!

RECORD 2

Most Athletics World Records Set on One Day

It took only 45 minutes for Jesse Owens to set 4 world records and earn the title **Most Athletics World Records Set on One Day**. On the afternoon of May 25, 1935, Owens started making history at a competition in Ann Arbor, Michigan, USA. He kicked off at 3:15 p.m. with the 100-yard dash in 9.4 seconds. A jaw-dropping 26 feet 8.25 inches long jump — a record that was unbroken for 25 years — came at 3:25 p.m. At 3:45 p.m., Owens blistered through the 220-yard dash in 20.3 seconds. Then he took the 220-yard low hurdles in 22.6 seconds at 4 p.m. to finish his awe-inspiring day.

FACT:

Florence Griffith-Joyner ran the Fastest Women's Outdoor 100 Meters in 10.49 seconds on July 16, 1998.

FLEET FEET

Records set before January 1977 were timed by stopwatch. A mere tenth of a second separated competitors. Electronic timers split the second into hundredths and, although introduced at the 1968 Mexico Olympics, these times were not officially accepted until later. Some historical highlights of the men's 100-meters:

- Jesse Owens dashed 10.2 seconds on June 20, 1936 — by stopwatch.
- Jim Hines sprinted 9.9 seconds on June 20, 1968 — by stopwatch.
- Jim Hines ran 9.95 seconds on October 14, 1968 — by electronic timer.
- Asafa Powell clocked in at 9.77 seconds on June 14, 2005 — by electronic timer.

FACT:

Jesse Owens broke the records in Michigan only 1 week after he had survived a bad fall down a flight of stairs.

Apnea means "without oxygen"!

RECORD 3

Constant Weight, Variable Weight & No Limits Free Diving

One breath can change your world.

Free diving, also known as apnea diving, requires staying underwater for as long as possible on one inhalation. Divers can go under with or without weights or fins, but they must complete their dive with just one breath of air! One of the relatively few sports in the world where gender is not a factor, free diving is definitely an endurance sport that requires intensive training of the mind and body, with some natural talent for holding your breath!

Englishwoman Tanya Streeter says it's the power of her mind and body that makes her a triple record-holder. On July 21, 2003, Streeter submerged off the Atlantic islands of Turks and Caicos and surfaced in the record books. Her free diving records and depths: **Constant Weight** (229 feet), **Variable Weight** (400 feet), and **No Limits** (525 feet). She has free dived to a depth of 400 feet – on a single breath that lasted an unfathomable 3 minutes 38 seconds! During the dive, her heart rate slowed to 15 beats per minute, her lungs compressed to the size of scrunched-up plastic bags, and her blood ceased to circulate around her extremities.

FACT:

Tanya Streeter began free diving at age 25. She has always loved the ocean, having grown up in the Grand Cayman Islands, Caribbean. A good snorkeler, she discovered her talent by chance.

RECORD 4

Most Snowboarding Championship Titles

Frenchwoman Karine Ruby won the Giant Slalom in 1996, the Snowboard Cross in 1997, and the 1998 Winter Olympics — this triple slam made her the record-holder for **Most Snowboarding Championship Titles**. She also holds the **Most Snowboarding World Cup Titles** — 16! Plus, Ruby has 2 Olympic medals: the 1998 gold and the 2002 silver in Parallel Giant Slalom, crowning her the women's record-holder for **Most Snowboarding Olympic Medals**. When not snowboard training, Ruby enjoys the rigorous sport of canyoning, where she navigates a canyon by foot, hand, rope, and raft.

SPARKLING RUBY

Athletes skate, ski, and — after an astonishing debut at the 1998 Winter Olympics in Nagano, Japan — snowboard for gold, silver, and bronze. Yet the non-Olympic Snowboard Cross is the true challenge for boarders. Four racers careen over a roller-coaster track, reaching speeds of 90 miles per hour while navigating curves, jumps, and drops. The most daring, and titled, racer is a woman named Karine Ruby, who is only 5 feet 4 inches tall and hails from Chamonix, France.

***Bails* and *craters* are board-speak for wild falls and crashes.**

Bored? Grab a board and get extreme!

What's the gnarliest feat done by professional skateboarder Danny Way? It's quite a list. Way started skating at age 6 and won his first competition at age 11. He's hit amazing heights (see the front cover), dropped from a helicopter onto a ramp, medaled at the X Games, been twice named Skateboarder of the Year, and jumped the Great Wall of China (see sidebar). At the top of the list are his dual Guinness World Records.

RECORD 5

Longest Skateboard Ramp Jump

On June 19, 2003, Danny Way grabbed big air and the record for **Highest Skateboard Air off a Quarter-Pipe** with a method air jump of 23 feet 6 inches, achieved off a 27-foot pipe at Point X Camp near Aguanga, California, USA. During the 2004 X Games X in Los Angeles, Way zipped down his Megaramp on August 8, 2004, and performed a 360. This was the **Longest Skateboard Ramp Jump** – mastering 79 feet, and breaking his 2002 world record of 65 feet set at Point X Camp. That's longer than three cars back-to-back!

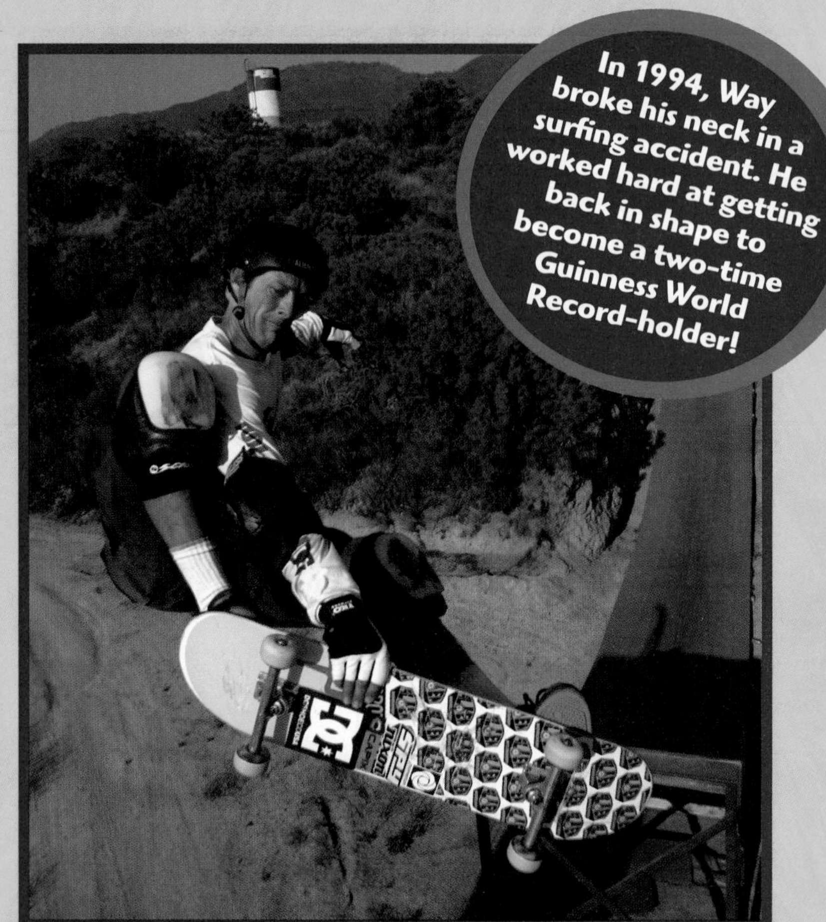

In 1994, Way broke his neck in a surfing accident. He worked hard at getting back in shape to become a two-time Guinness World Record-holder!

WAY TO WALL

Danny Way jumped over the Great Wall of China on July 9, 2005! Built 2,300 years ago to keep out invading tribes, the Great Wall is 1,500 miles long. While others tried and some died during previous attempts, Way cleared the wall 5 times! This effort took extensive planning and training. Way's team constructed a Megaramp near Beijing, China for his launch point. He reached over 50 miles per hour on the ramp to clear the shocking 61-foot gap, before landing safely. Although he hit amazing heights, Way did not break his other records because he lost control of his skateboard.

FACT:

The "method air" jump is considered a straightforward jump, but don't try it at home. Your front hand grabs a heel edge, bend your knees, and pull the board up behind you — to the level of your head!

Mighty Marathons

Ever since that first grueling marathon in ancient Greece, people have admired those individuals able to excel at, and endure, journeys of great distances. In this section, we'll pedal in a 20-day bike race, keep pace with a weekly marathon man, and trek between poles. Do your feet ache? Go for a spin inside a zorb, or fly off on a trip around the world!

Some people have to see for themselves that the Earth really *is* round!

A self-made millionaire turned adventurer, American Steve Fossett enjoys going around our planet by balloon, boat, and plane. Jules Verne's *Around the World in 80 Days* must have inspired his first global trip. From June 19 to July 2, 2002, he piloted his hot air balloon, *Spirit of Freedom*, in a 20,626-mile trip of 13 days 8 hours 33 minutes for the First Solo Around-the-World Balloon Trip (see photos on pages 3 and 45).

RECORD 6

First Solo Circumnavigation by Aircraft without Refueling

From March 1 through March 3, 2005, aviator Steve Fossett completed the **First Solo Circumnavigation by Aircraft without Refueling**, by taking off and landing in Salina, Kansas, USA. The *GlobalFlyer*, specifically designed for this trip, was made of superlight composite materials. Its total weight was 22,100 pounds, of which 11,000 pounds was fuel. The cockpit size was 7 feet 7 inches in a single-engine, single-pilot turbofan aircraft. Not a lot of room to maneuver during his trip of 67 hours 1 minute!

Courageous Lance Armstrong is an icon of inspiration!

As a child athlete in Plano, Texas, Armstrong displayed a natural talent and competitive heart for cycling. He won an Iron Kids Triathlon at age 13 then zipped through the amateur ranks to turn pro by age 16! By 1996, Armstrong had competed in the Atlanta Summer Olympics, achieved a #1 world ranking, and signed with a famous French racing team. Pain cut short a race and revealed Armstrong had cancer. He battled his way back to a full recovery in 1998. His comeback from such adversity was in itself an inspiration, but Armstrong wanted to get back on that saddle and win again.

RECORD 7

Most Tour de France Wins

In 1999, Lance Armstrong's goal was simply to finish the world-famous Tour de France. Not only did he finish, he won the race! His win was a result of sheer power, aggressiveness, and team strategy. Armstrong was truly back on top and continued to win the Tour a phenomenal 6 more times (2000–2005). There have been five other cyclists who won 5 times, but Armstrong is ahead of the pack with his 7 consecutive triumphs – and a Guinness World Record for **Most Tour de France Wins**.

Why is Armstrong such a cycling superstar? He is a great all-around rider who is equally talented on the flat stages, in individual and team time trials, and on mountainous terrain. It is said that the Tour is won and lost in the mountains, and clearly Armstrong, who is known as a detailed preparer, is ready for everything!

Lance Armstrong's resting heart rate is only 32 – 34 beats per minute. An average person's resting heart rate is 50 – 90 beats per minute.

FACT:

Traditionally at a mountain summit, spectators give the riders newspapers to tuck under their jerseys for insulation during the cold descent.

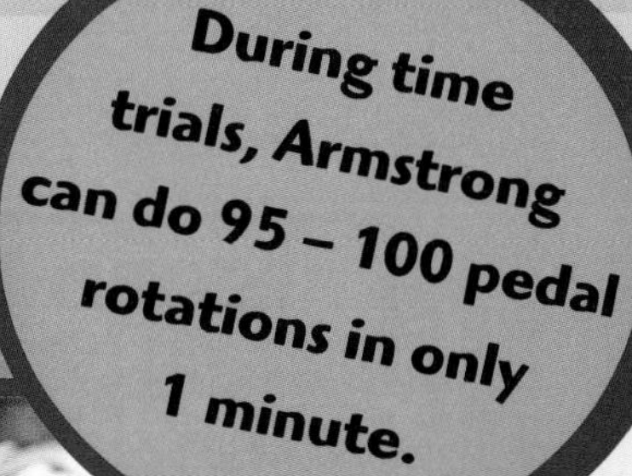

During time trials, Armstrong can do 95 – 100 pedal rotations in only 1 minute.

UP CLOSE

A TOUGH TOUR

The Tour de France began in 1903 and continues to be one of the most intense athletic events in the world. Every July, the approximately 3,500-kilometer race has a different route, broken up into approximately 20 stages. The route always includes the Alps and Pyrenees mountains and traditionally ends on Paris' famous Champs Elysées boulevard.

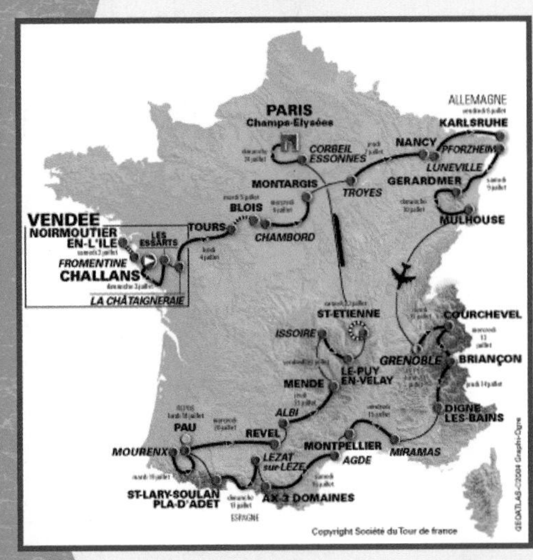

Completing the journey, regardless of the mileage, is the goal.

Headed out on an expedition? Call Sir Ranulph Fiennes, the world explorer who likes to boldly go everywhere. In his spare time, he writes books, gives lectures, runs marathons, and finds lost cities. Fiennes discovered the ancient city Ubar, which had not been seen since 300 AD, in the Arabian deserts of Oman. His search lasted 26 years, with 7 separate expeditions, spanning 1968 to 1991. Ubar is now the biggest archaeological site in the Middle East. Let's explore this intrepid globetrotter's life.

RECORD 8

First Pole-to-Pole Circumnavigation

In 1982, Sir Ranulph Fiennes — alongside Charles Burton and his Parson's terrier, Bothie — completed a 3-year, 52,000 mile expedition between the North and South poles for the **First Pole-to-Pole Circumnavigation**. Before that trip, he took 55 days — from October 28, 1980 to January 11, 1981 — to finish the 2,600-mile transantarctic leg of the 1980-1982 Trans-Globe Expedition from Sanae to Scott Base. Charles Burton and Oliver Shepard trekked with him. In 1993, Dr. Michael Stroud logged 1,350 miles in 94 days alongside Fiennes for the **Longest Self-Supporting Trek**. Each man dragged a 500-pound supply sledge. This trip was also the **Longest Unsupported Antarctic Trek Ever** and the **Fastest Antarctic Crossing**.

FACT:

Fiennes also ran 7 marathons on all 7 continents within 7 days in 2003, after undergoing bypass surgery. That's what we call a lot of "get up and go!"

RECORD 9

Most Consecutive Weekends of Marathon Running

Unlike Sir Ranulph Fiennes, Richard Worley (not pictured) didn't plan on running a marathon. During a visit with a college buddy, he tagged along on a race although he had never run in one before. Worley finished in 4 hours 8 minutes, and a marathon man was born. To get ready for his 50th birthday, he decided to challenge himself by running in at least one marathon every week! Worley ran a marathon or an ultramarathon (a race longer than the regulation 26.2 miles of a marathon) every weekend from January 5, 1997 to January 16, 2000. His dedication resulted in the **Most Consecutive Weekends of Marathon Running** (159)! For the exhaustive total of races run, sprint over to the sidebar.

MARATHON MAN

Richard Worley made sure the scenery wasn't boring during his races! He simultaneously joined the 50 States Marathon Club by running a marathon in each and every one of the 50 states, plus the District of Columbia, in one calendar year. He managed this feat every year for 3 years — 1997, 1998, and 1999. His mileage actually totals to 200 marathons completed. He was willing to go that extra mile in life!

Worley's first race of his record: Walt Disney World Marathon in Orlando, Florida. His last race: Houston Methodist Marathon in Houston, Texas.

A zorb rider is a zorbonaut.

If you re-invented the wheel, would you go for a spin inside it?

About 15 years ago, two New Zealanders constructed a ball large enough to fit a human passenger inside. The zorb ball is made of two layers of specially designed inflatable rubber, and can roll across water and land. It's about 11 feet in diameter and weighs almost 198 pounds (without a rider). Between the two layers is a 2-foot cushion of air. This air cushion and a harness allow riders to safely roll, and bounce, downhill in the sport of zorbing. A rider makes one complete rotation every 30 feet. The trip is said to not be as stomach churning as it looks!

RECORD 10

Greatest Distance Zorbing

Richard Eley of the UK (not pictured) secured the Guinness World Record for the **Greatest Distance Zorbing** in one roll. On May 10, 1999, Eley reached a speed of 31 miles per hour — that's almost as fast as a racehorse — during his 1,059 feet 8.5 inches record-setting roll near Glynde, East Sussex, UK.

FACT:

Riders can be from age 6 to 89. Only three balls (maximum 540 pounds) can zorb in the same area at the same time!

UP CLOSE

SPIN DRY

Zorbing is the zany sport of rolling down a hill inside a giant, inflatable ball. After the zorb ball is inflated, it is positioned at the top of a steep hill. The rider climbs inside and fastens a safety harness. Someone outside gives a good push, and off you roll!

There are two ways to zorb.

- A "dry" zorb is a standard ride.

- Just add water inside for a "wet" (or "hydro") zorb. The rider tries to keep upright inside the rolling — and sloshing — ball. Riders can spin dry on the next trip!

It takes about 5 minutes to blow up a zorb using a leaf blower!

Part of Art

Artistic talent is displayed in unexpected ways. Inside this book, we can sit beside some of the world's greatest artists. Yet art isn't always expressed by paint on a canvas or located in a museum — wait until you see what can happen with pumpkins, balloons, or your own body. Art is beautiful, interesting, and can even catch criminals!

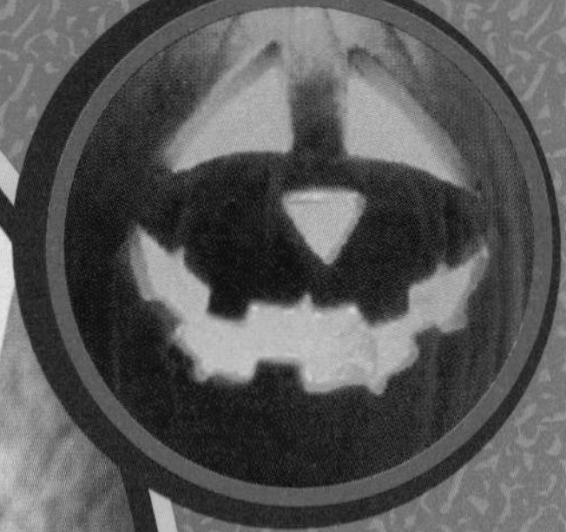

UP CLOSE

RECORD 11

Most Tattooed Man

Scientists believe tattooing may have been practiced before 8,000 BCE — that's around the last Ice Age! The oldest known tattooed body is of a Bronze Age man, more than 5,000 years old, discovered in a glacier in the mountains near Austria. People have continued the traditional art of decorating their bodies with ink. Tom Leppard (pictured) and Lucky Rich share the artistic-expression record for **Most Tattooed Man**. Tattoos cover an amazing 99.9 percent of their bodies! Rich "blacked over" his previous tattoos as a background for an intricate design in white ink. Leppard chose a leopard-skin design as his permanent bodysuit. The only art-free areas are between his toes and inside his ears.

COUNTED OUT

Body tattoo competitions have rules. Tattoo judging used to be done by simply counting the number of tattoos a person had on their body. But competitors began adding tiny dots, and the rules were changed to reflect the highest percentage of body coverage on an individual. This way, both smaller and larger-size people can compete on equal footing.

FACT:

The word pumpkin grew from pepon, Greek for "large melon." The French transformed pepon into pompon, before handing it to the English to become pumpion. American colonists then carved out their own variation of pumpkin.

Tools used by the artist are brushes, chisels, and imagination.

Sixth-grade school teacher Stephen Clarke started his gourd-fascination in childhood. The fifth of nine children, Clarke usually cleaned out the pumpkin seeds instead of carving at Halloween. The chore taught him about gardening. Years later, he won first place for his pumpkin-and-squash harvest basket and spent his prize money on a pumpkin-carving kit! Today he frequently has orange-colored hands. It's a hazard of his record-setting skill.

RECORD 12

Fastest Pumpkin Carver

The **Fastest Pumpkin Carver** sliced through the records in 54.72 seconds on October 23, 2001, at the Camden City Children's Garden, New Jersey, USA. A single jack-o'-lantern by Stephen Clarke shattered his own previous record of 1 minute 14.8 seconds. Not content with a mere speed record, Clarke showcased his stamina during a live TV broadcast of *The Early Show*, where he set the record for **Most Pumpkins Carved in One Hour** – 42 gourds – on October 31, 2002. People travel to see the Clarke family's annual Halloween display, which includes jack-o'-lantern faces of Mona Lisa, Humphrey Bogart, and Mt. Rushmore. It takes Clarke no time at all to decorate for Halloween.

RECORD 13

Most Balloon Sculptures Made in One Hour

Are you good at twisting balloons into wacky shapes? Maybe with a serious amount of practice and a nose for competition, you can challenge John Cassidy in a balloon blow-off! Agile and accurate Cassidy is the current record-holder for **Most Balloon Sculptures Made in One Hour**. Cassidy made 529 inflatable sculptures, shaped by his breath and nimble fingers, on October 14, 2003, in New York City, USA. On average, Cassidy sculpted a balloon every 6.8 seconds!

RULES OF THE ROUND

For budding balloon competitors, here are some rules of the "round:"

- **All balloons must be mouth-blown — no pumps allowed!**
- **No substitute blowers. Only the competitor's mouth and lungs allowed.**
- **A 60-minute competition limit, with no extensions!**
- **A minimum of 30 different shapes must be completed.**

So if a dog is the sole shape in your repertoire, you can't simply make 600 balloon dogs in a row!

"Every child is an artist. The problem is how to remain an artist once he grows up."

This quote is by the famous painter known as Picasso. Pablo Diego José Francisco de Paula Juan Nepomuceno de los Remedios Crispín Cipriano de la Santísima Trinidad Ruíz y Picasso was born in 1881. He shortened his tongue twister of a name to "Pablo Picasso." Because he lived until age 91 and kept creating works of art throughout his life, millions of people all over the world have seen his pieces in museums, books, magazines, and on television.

RECORD 14
Most Prolific Painter

Picasso was innovative, even painting his sister's portrait in egg yolk as a kid! He constantly used fresh methods to express his vision. He liked to work in many different mediums — painting, drawing, sculpture, ceramics, collage, and illustration. He was the **Most Prolific Painter** in a career that lasted 75 years and resulted in 13,500 paintings! That's one painting every two days! He created more than 100,000 prints and engravings, 34,000 book illustrations, and 300 sculptures and ceramics.

UP CLOSE

FACT:

Picasso invented Cubism, a painting style that reflects different points of view in one picture surface. Traditional African and Oceanic masks and art served as inspiration for this style.

PRICEY PAINT

Many famous artworks are owned by museums and are never sold to private buyers. But works of art by Picasso have been sold at auction no fewer than 3,579 times. By May 9, 1997, this number hit the record for Most Auction Sales by an Artist! His reputation as the most important artist of the 20th century was enhanced by another recent auction. *Garçon à la Pipe,* painted in 1905 when Picasso was 24, was originally bought in Paris for $30,000 in 1950. A 2004 auction at Sotheby's resulted in the painting's sale for $104 million ($93 million plus premium and fees).

Portrait artist Lois Gibson was drawn to justice.

A survivor of a violent crime at age 21, Gibson saw her attacker arrested. Her experience inspired her to help others in their pursuit of justice. A self-trained forensics artist, Gibson has a Fine Arts degree from the University of Texas at Austin. She had drawn more than 3,000 tourist portraits before approaching the Houston Police Department with pencil in hand. Today, she balances being the teacher of a forensics art course at Northwestern University with capturing criminals on paper.

RECORD 15

Most Criminals Positively Identified Due to the Composite of One Artist

Many artists create their images from real-life models. However, Lois Gibson does not need the subjects of her portrait sketches to sit still for her. Instead, she creates composite images of a criminal's face based on descriptions from the victims and witnesses of their crimes. Gibson is only one of 19 full-time forensics artists in the USA, but she's the record-holder for **Most Criminals Positively Identified Due to the Composite of One Artist**. Since 1982, more than 158 criminals have been identified and brought to justice in Texas as a result of Gibson's portraits.

FACT:

Lois Gibson's sketches nab criminals 30 percent of the time.

Ageless

These record-setters didn't let their calendar age dictate what they could or couldn't do. Meet a versatile actor and the youngest writer-director-producer of the silver screen, a young king and an aged queen, plus a boy who became a medical doctor at age 17!

Moviemaking fascinates story-tellers of all ages.

Highlights in cinematic history:

2,500 BCE Sitting in a dark room, Chinese philosopher Mo-Ti ponders an upside-down image of the outside world projected onto the wall through a hole in the opposite wall.

1490 Leonardo da Vinci describes an image-projecting machine.

1671 Athanasius Kircher invents the "Magic Lantern" — an oil lamp, a lens, and painted glass plates.

1880 Eadweard Muybridge projects his serial photography of a running horse.

1895 The first motion picture, *The Arrival of a Train* by the Lumière brothers, premieres at the Grand Café in Paris, France.

RECORD 16

Youngest Film Director-Writer-Producer

Sydney Ling (not pictured) liked to tell stories at an early age. By the time he was 13, he had told an original story on film and earned the Guinness World Record for **Youngest Film Director-Writer-Producer**. His feature-length movie, *Lex the Wonder Dog*, was released in 1973. The thriller about a canine detective played on movie screens in the Netherlands. Can you guess the lead actor? That was Sydney Ling, too!

FACT:

A feature-length script is approximately 100 to 120 pages. The filmmaker's formula: 1 page of script = 1 minute of film time.

In the 1950s, Christopher Lee met J. R. R. Tolkien, author of *The Lord of the Rings* books.

UP CLOSE

RECORD 17

Living Actor with Most Screen Credits

Actor Christopher Lee has appeared on the silver screen an astonishing 211 times — and he's still working! Since his debut in 1948, Lee's piercing eyes, resonant voice, and impressive height have scared and thrilled movie audiences around the world. In his 80s, Lee starred in two motion picture sagas: as Saruman the White, the good wizard gone bad, in *The Lord of the Rings* films; and as the mysterious Count Dooku in the second and third *Star Wars* prequels. Lee continues to enjoy bringing characters to life, making him the record-holder for the **Living Actor with Most Screen Credits**.

ACTING CHOPS

Born Christopher Frank Caradini Lee on May 27, 1922, in London, England, this distinguished actor speaks Russian, Italian, French, Spanish, and German, in addition to his native English. However, being 6 feet 5 inches tall made casting a challenge, so he took small roles until he "went evil." At age 35, Lee starred as the Creature in *Curse of Frankenstein*. His villainous roles include several star turns as Count Dracula and Fu Manchu. Lee also did his own stunts. He is an accomplished screen swordfighter but got stabbed in the knee during the making of *The Three Musketeers*.

Monarchy is one of the oldest types of government.

Monarchs were once the heads of state and had absolute control over everything that happened in their countries or states. These absolute monarchies were based on hereditary succession, and the monarch usually ruled for life. The czar and czarinas of Russia, the kings and queens of Europe, the emperor and empresses of China were all absolute monarchs in their time.

Today, most monarchies are constitutional monarchies, which means elected officials are the true heads of the government.

King Mswati III was named Makhosetive, the Siswati word for "King of All Nations." Siswati is the official language of Swaziland.

RECORD 18

Youngest Reigning Monarch

King Mswati III is the only absolute monarch in sub-Saharan Africa. He was crowned on April 25, 1986, at the age of 18 years 6 days. He is the **Youngest Reigning Monarch**. Swaziland is an independent country, populated by 1.17 million people, in the southern part of Africa. South Africa and Mozambique form its borders, and it is about two-thirds the size of New Jersey. The country was formed in 1881 as a haven for tribes fleeing from the Zulus, but it did not gain independence until 1968.

RECORD 19

Longest Reigning Queen

The title for the **Longest Reigning Queen** belongs to Victoria, Queen of Great Britain (1837 – 1901) and Empress of India from 1876 until her death in 1901. Her monarchy lasted 63 years and 216 days. She, like King Mswati III, was 18 when she became queen after the death of her uncle, King William IV, who had no other legitimate heirs. Just before Victoria took the throne, England made the formal transition from absolute monarchy to constitutional monarchy. Nevertheless, Queen Victoria was closely involved in political decisions. She had few actual powers but wielded a lot of influence on the prime ministers. She encouraged peace and reconciliation in world affairs.

A TIMELY REIGN

The Victorian Era, as it's now known, was a time of enormous scientific and industrial change. Follow the crowns to see the world's transformation during Victoria's reign.

- **Gold and diamonds were discovered in Africa.**
- **Lightbulbs, photography, telephones, and motorcars were invented.**
- **The first public libraries were opened.**
- **Queen Victoria was the first reigning monarch to travel by railway car!**

FACT:

Victoria was the great-great-great-great-grandmother of princes William and Harry of England.

College graduates usually earn a degree in four years, but not these educational record-breakers.

Mozelle Richardson is the Oldest Graduate at the age of 90 years 103 days. She started her studies in the fall semester of 1967. Over the next three decades, she kept studying and writing. On May 8, 2004, Richardson graduated from the University of Oklahoma Gaylord College of Journalism and Mass Communication, USA. She had earned her Bachelor of Arts degree in Journalism. Her dedication also resulted in 6 published books!

RECORD 20

Youngest Physician

Child prodigies are those whose outstanding talent comes at a young age, such as Mozart. American Balamurali Ambati was born in 1977, finished high school at age 11, and graduated from New York University at age 13! Ambati went on to graduate from the Mount Sinai School of Medicine in New York City on May 19, 1995, at 17 years 294 days — making him the **Youngest Physician** ever in the world. Today, Dr. Ambati is an opthalmologist and corneal specialist at the Medical College of Georgia.

Best Of . . .

Five of our favorite record-holders have amazed and amused audiences throughout the years. Walk a day in the shoes of a classic Guinness World Records superstar. Learn how a boy believed in himself enough to become the record-holder for having the most records. Find out how a construction worker moved bricks to become a multiple world record-holder. See a fearless man catch, bathe, and balance rattlesnakes! Then measure a bubble blown by the queen of bubblegum bubbles.

Going to the movies meant calling in advance. Wadlow needed five seats across and a few rows, too!

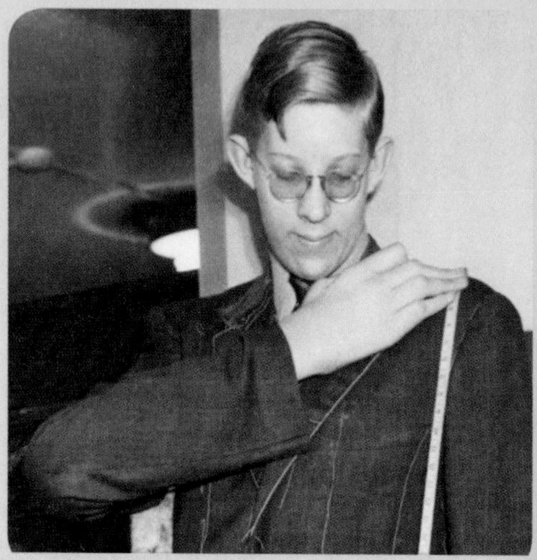

The "Gentle Giant" lived his life in size extra-large.

Born on February 22, 1918, Robert Pershing Wadlow weighed 8 pounds 5 ounces. Like his parents, two younger brothers, and sisters, he began life normal-sized. Within a few years, Wadlow's natural growth became an international story.

RECORD 21

Tallest Man Ever

Guinness World Records requires three height measurements within a 24-hour period for the record to be certified. The **Tallest Man Ever** stood 8 feet 11.1 inches tall, and weighed 439 pounds, during his last measurement on June 27, 1940. When Robert Pershing Wadlow was 12, it was determined that he had an overactive pituitary gland that caused his astounding growth. These days, there are treatments for such a condition, but in the 1920s, there was no safe therapy available. Generally, Wadlow was in good health, except for his feet, in which he had limited sensation. A blister in one of his feet led to a fatal infection. The Gentle Giant died July 15, 1940 at age 22. More than 40,000 people paid their respects at his funeral. A lifelong resident of Alton, Illinois, he was buried in the Oakwood Cemetery and his inscription reads, "At Rest."

37AA Shoes = 18.5 inches long.

A GROWTH CHART

Trace Robert Pershing Wadlow's growth throughout his life.

AGE	HEIGHT	WEIGHT
5 years	5 feet 4 inches	105 pounds
8 years	6 feet	169 pounds
10 years	6 feet 5 inches	210 pounds
14 years	7 feet 5 inches	301 pounds
16 years	7 feet 10.24 inches	374 pounds
17 years	8 feet 0.38 inches	315 pounds
19 years	8 feet 5.5 inches	480 pounds
21 years	8 feet 8.25 inches	491 pounds
22.4 years	8 feet 11.1 inches	439 pounds

FACT:

Wadlow's hands measured 12.75 inches from the wrist to the tip of his middle finger. Size 25 was his ring size!

Most Glasses Balanced on Chin: 75 pint glasses for 10.6 seconds on April 26, 2001.

If you believe in yourself, the impossible will become possible.

Ashrita Furman is the undisputed Guinness World Record champion par excellence! Furman got into improving his physical capabilities after studying meditation with Indian holy man, Sri Chinmoy. He was inspired by teachings about the fulfillment of human potential. His first certified Guinness World Record was 27,000 consecutive jumping jacks in 6 hours 45 minutes in 1979.

Ashrita Furman's attitude toward competition: " I'm not going against any person, but against the ideal. When someone breaks one of my records, I'm happy because he's just raised the bar and, in some way, increased the level of progress of humanity."

RECORD 22

Most Prolific Record-Breaker

The **Most Prolific Record-Breaker** hails from Jamaica, New York, USA, and says he was a complete nerd in high school. Ashrita Furman still does not consider himself a "natural athlete." A 50-year-old health-food-store manager, he has set or broken more than 80 official Guinness World Records and is the holder of the most current standing records — 26. As if this isn't enough, Furman also holds the record for **Most Individual Records**.

Greatest Distance Walked with a Milk Bottle Balanced on the Head: 80.96 miles in 23 hours 35 minutes on April 22–23, 1998.

GLOBE TROTTING

Ashrita Furman has set records on all seven continents, including Antarctica. Let's take a record-setting tour:

- **August 23, 2001 — Most underwater rope jumps in one hour set in Montawk, USA (900 jumps, 60 minutes).**
- **July 23, 1999 — Fastest time to pogo stick up Canada's CN Tower (1,899 steps, 57 minutes 51 seconds).**
- **May 31, 2004 — Race walking the fastest mile while hula hooping in Moscow, Russia (14 minutes 25 seconds).**
- **January 12-13, 1998 — Playing hopscotch for 24 hours straight in Cancún, Mexico (434 games in 24 hours).**

Breaking records takes confidence, concentration, and a headstrong attitude.

John Evans is solidly built, but his true strength resides in his determined heart and his incredibly strong neck. Evans discovered his load-carrying capacity while working on a building site at age 18. His pay was linked to the amount of bricks carried. He found he could carry double the amount by balancing bricks on his head using a special hat, called a "hod." This was the first in a series of incredible balancing acts that made Evans a superstar in the record books.

UP CLOSE

RECORD 23

Greatest Weight Balanced on the Head

The **Greatest Weight Balanced on the Head** was 101 bricks totaling a weight of 416 pounds. John Evans balanced the load for 10 seconds (pictured on page 35). The event occurred at the BBC Television Centre in London, England, on December 24, 1997. Professional headbalancer Evans holds records in balancing many items — including milk crates, footballs, people, and a car. Nor can anyone overlook the **Most Books Balanced on the Head** (above). There were 62 identical *Guinness World Records* books stacked in a single column — 217 pounds and 73 inches high — that Evans kept aloft at Abbeydale, Sheffield, UK, on December 9, 1998!

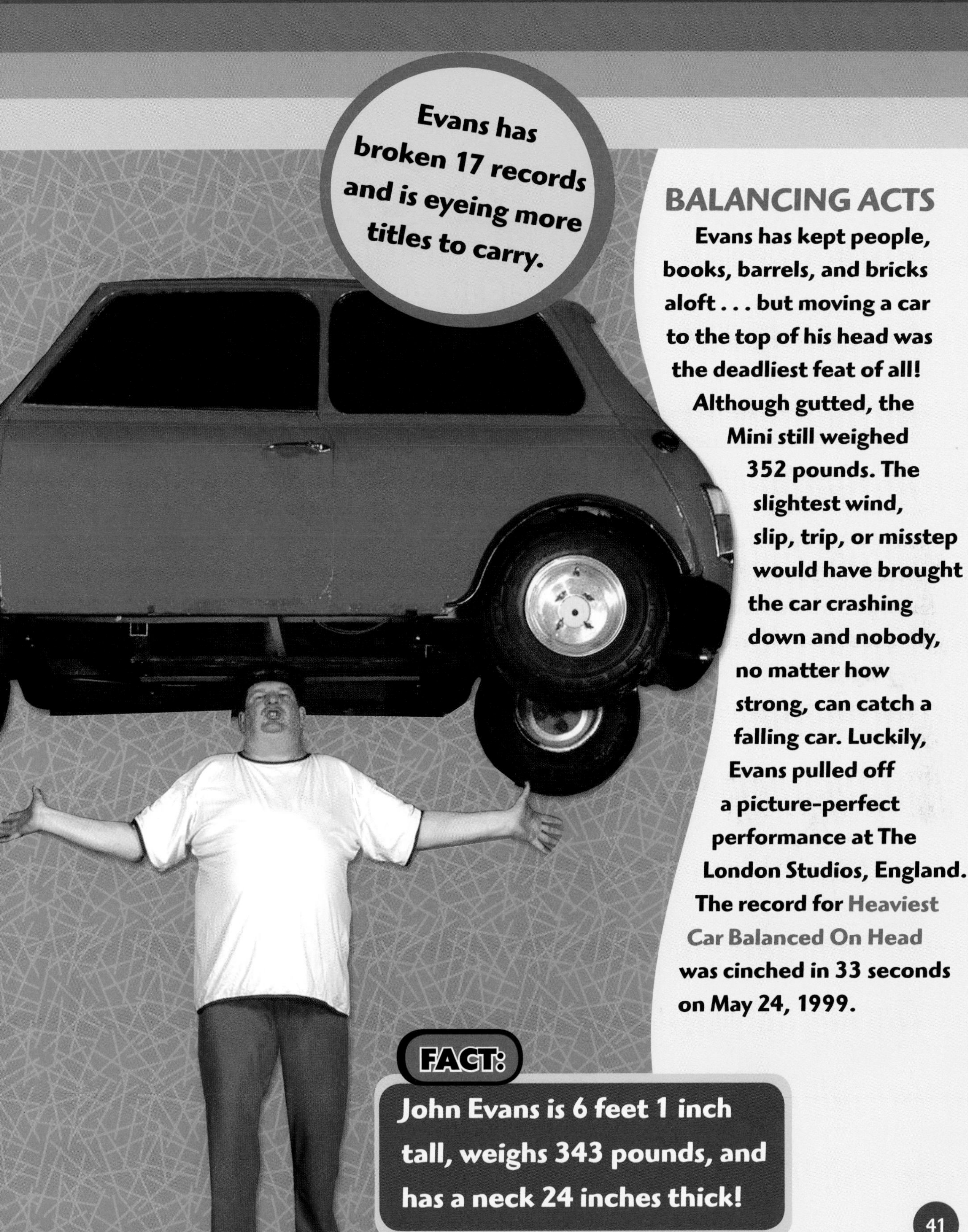

Evans has broken 17 records and is eyeing more titles to carry.

BALANCING ACTS

Evans has kept people, books, barrels, and bricks aloft . . . but moving a car to the top of his head was the deadliest feat of all! Although gutted, the Mini still weighed 352 pounds. The slightest wind, slip, trip, or misstep would have brought the car crashing down and nobody, no matter how strong, can catch a falling car. Luckily, Evans pulled off a picture-perfect performance at The London Studios, England. The record for Heaviest Car Balanced On Head was cinched in 33 seconds on May 24, 1999.

FACT:

John Evans is 6 feet 1 inch tall, weighs 343 pounds, and has a neck 24 inches thick!

Do you know a snake charmer?

Whether bathing, sleeping, dressing, or walking, this man is fearless around rattlesnakes. Jackie Bibby, also known as "The Texas Snake Man," has been chilling out with his cold-blooded reptilian rattlers for several years. Guinness World Records caught a slew of slithery tales from Bibby's fright-inducing feats.

Bibby has been bitten 8 times seriously enough for hospital stays. He's also lost half a thumb.

RECORD 24

Most Live Rattlesnakes Held in the Mouth

Jackie Bibby performed his most jaw-dropping act during the Guinness World Records Experience in Orlando, Florida, on May 19, 2001. Careful not to bite down or to be bitten, Bibby dangled 8 live rattlesnakes by their tails from his mouth for 12.5 seconds. He clearly earned the record for **Most Live Rattlesnakes Held in the Mouth**.

Bibby's recreational activities include **Sharing a Bathtub with the Most Rattlesnakes**. He has sat with 75 Western Diamondback rattlesnakes in one bathtub. This record was set in Los Angeles, California, USA, during the taping of the TV show *Guinness World Records: Primetime* on September 24, 1999.

RATTLESNAKE ROUNDUP

Every spring, Texas' ranchers clear their land of snakes. This chore eventually became a competition named the Rattlesnake Roundup that Jackie Bibby has participated in. How do you sack snakes safely (and say that five times fast without spitting)? One person is in charge of a burlap sack. The other person picks up snakes.

The team tries to get all 10 of the slithery hissers up and into the sack as fast as possible — and not get bitten!

Blowing bubbles is a tradition floating throughout history.

Pop through bubblegum's highlights:

- **50 AD Greeks chew mastiche, tree resin from mastic tree**
- **1848 First commercial "spruce gum" made by John Curtis from Bradford, Maine, USA**
- **1869 Dentist William Finley Semple from Mount Vernon, Ohio, USA, gets first patent for "chewing-gum"**
- **1906 Frank Fleer invents bubble gum, called Blibber Blabber, but it's too sticky**
- **1928 Walter Diemer, accountant, invents modern bubble gum — named Dubble Bubble**

RECORD 25

Largest Bubblegum Bubble Blown

Susan Montgomery Williams of Fresno, California, USA, is the reigning bubblegum-blowing queen. She holds the unpopped record for **Largest Bubblegum Bubble Blown** — 23 inches in diameter. That's bigger than a basketball!

With 15 years of oversize bubble production behind her, Williams was a shoo-in to set the record. After all, she had already done it 3 times before. Her first record came in 1979 when friends sent her cross-country to Jacksonville, Florida, for a Bubble Yum Gum contest. Willams' friends were right, because she won first place with a 19-inch super-size bubble! For her record-making blow, she used three pieces of Bubble Yum Gum on July 19, 1994, at the ABC-TV studios in New York City. Where will you make your bubblegum-blowing debut?

There are more than 1,000 kinds of gum sold in the USA.

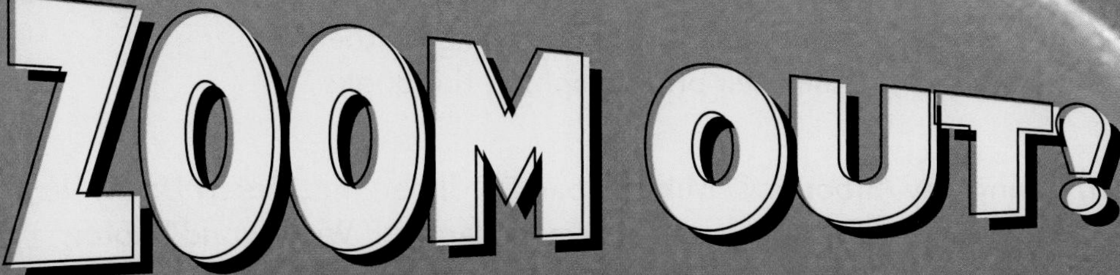

ZOOM OUT!

Although our book ends here, your exploration of these incredible people and their record-setting stories can continue among the online archives (www.guinnessworldrecords.com) and within the pages of *Guinness World Records*.

Go up close and get involved — it's your world!

Photo Credits

The publisher would like to thank the following for their kind permission to use their photographs in this book:

Cover, title page (main) Danny Way Airborne © Mike Blabac/DC Shoes, Inc., (inset) Danny Way © Peter Parks/AFP/Getty Images; 3 Steve Fossett © Steve Holland/AP Wide World Photos; 4 Grouse © Tom Vezo/Peter Arnold, Inc.; 5 (main) Karine Ruby © Reuters/CORBIS, (top) Jesse Owens © Bettmann/CORBIS, (bottom) Tanya Streeter © Dan Burton/AP Wide World Photos; 6 Richard Petty's Racecar © Jeff Gross/Getty Images; 7 Richard Petty © Harry Reiter/Reuters, Lawn Mower Racing © Phillippe Hays/REX USA; 8 Jesse Owens © AP Wide World Photos; 9 Florence Griffith-Joyner © AFP/Getty Images; 10 Tanya Streeter © Reuters/CORBIS; 11 Karine Ruby © Peter DeJong/AP Wide World Photos; 12 Danny Way Skates Megaramp © Donald Miralle/ Getty Images; 13 (top) Danny Way in China © Mike Blabac/Quiksilver/DC via Getty Images, (bottom) Danny Way Airborne © Ric Francis/AP Wide World Photos; 14 (left), 20, 21 Zorbing © Zorb Ltd. 2005; 14 (main) Lance Armstrong © John Pierce/REX USA, (right) Sir Ranulph Fiennes © Will Burgess/Reuters; 15 Steve Fossett © Steve Bell/REX USA, (inset) GlobalFlyer © Thierry Boccon-Gibod-Pool/Getty Images; 17 Lance Armstrong © Franck Fife/AP Wide World Photos, (inset) Armstrong Races © Eric Gaillard/Reuters, Tour de France Map © Société du Tour de France/AP Wide World Photos; 18 Sir Ranulph Fiennes © Graham Chadwick/Getty Images; 19 Marathon Runners © Bizuayehu Tesfaye/AP Wide World Photos; 22 (main) Canvas © Comstock/PictureQuest, (top) Pumpkin © Photodisc via SODA, (bottom) Tattoos © Reuters; 23 Tom Leppard © Ian Waldie/REX USA; 24 Stephen Clarke © 2005 Drew Gardner/Guinness World Records; 25 John Cassidy © Richard Faverty/Beckett Studios/Courtesy of John Cassidy, (inset) Dog Balloon Sculpture © Chapman Baxter/Courtesy of John Cassidy; 26 Pablo Picasso © George Stroud/Hulton Archive/Getty Images; 27 Picasso in Studio © Arnold Newman/Getty Images; 28 Lois Gibson, Forensics Portrait © David J. Phillip/AP Wide World Photos; 29 (left) King Mswati III © AP Wide World Photos, (main) Queen Victoria © AP Wide World Photos, (right) Christopher Lee © Russell Boyce/Reuters; 30 Filmmaker © Creatas/PictureQuest; 31 Lord of the Rings © New Line Cinema/Photofest, (inset) Christopher Lee © Charles Platiau/ Reuters; 32 King Mswati III © Themba Hadebe/AP Wide World Photos; 33 Queen Victoria, (inset) Painting © Hulton Archive/Getty Images; 34 Mozelle Richardson © Sean P. Steffen/ Courtesy of Mozelle Richardson, Dr. Ambati © Kathy Willens/AP Wide World Photos; 35 Jackie Bibby © Ellis Neel/Almogordo Daily News/AP Wide World Photos; 35 (left), 38, 39 Ashrita Furman © 2004 Drew Gardner/Guinness World Records; 35 (right), 41 John Evans © 2001 Drew Gardner/Guinness World Records; 36 Robert Pershing Wadlow © Bettmann/ CORBIS; 40 John Evans Balancing Books Courtesy of John Evans, www.headbalancer.com; 42, 43 Jackie Bibby© 2005 Drew Gardner/Guinness World Records; 44 Susan Montgomery-Williams Courtesy of Susan Montgomery-Williams; 45 Steve Fossett's Balloon © Reuters.

Message from the Keeper of the Records:

Record-breakers are the ultimate in one way or another — the youngest, the oldest, the tallest, the smallest. So how do you get to be a record-breaker? Follow these important steps:

1. Before you attempt your record, check with us to make sure your record is suitable and safe. Get your parents' permission. Next, contact one of our officials by using the record application form at www.guinnessworldrecords.com.

2. Tell us about your idea. Give us as much information as you can, including what the record is, when you want to attempt it, where you'll be doing it, and other relevant information.
   a) We will tell you if a record already exists, what safety guidelines you must follow during your attempt to break that record, and what evidence we need as proof that you completed your attempt.
   b) If your idea is a brand-new record nobody has set yet, we need to make sure it meets our requirements. If it does, then we'll write official rules and safety guidelines specific to that record idea and make sure all attempts are made in the same way.

3. Whether it is a new or existing record, we will send you the guidelines for your selected record. Once you receive these, you can make your attempt at any time. You do not need a Guinness World Record official at your attempt. But you do need to gather evidence. Find out more about the kind of evidence we need to see by visiting our website.

4. Think you've already set or broken a record? Put all of your evidence as specified by the guidelines in an envelope and mail it to us at: Guinness World Records, 338 Euston Road, London NWI 38D UK.

5. Our officials will investigate your claim fully — a process that can take up to a few weeks, depending on the number of claims we've received, and how complex your record is.

6. If you're successful, you will receive an official certificate that says you are now a Guinness World Record-holder!

Need more info? Check out the Kids' Zone on www.guinnessworldrecords.com for lots more hints, tips, and top record ideas that you can try at home or at school. Good luck!

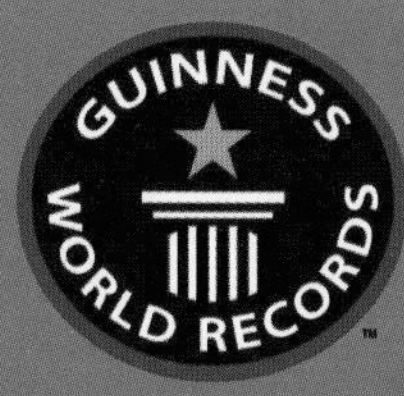
GUINNESS WORLD RECORDS

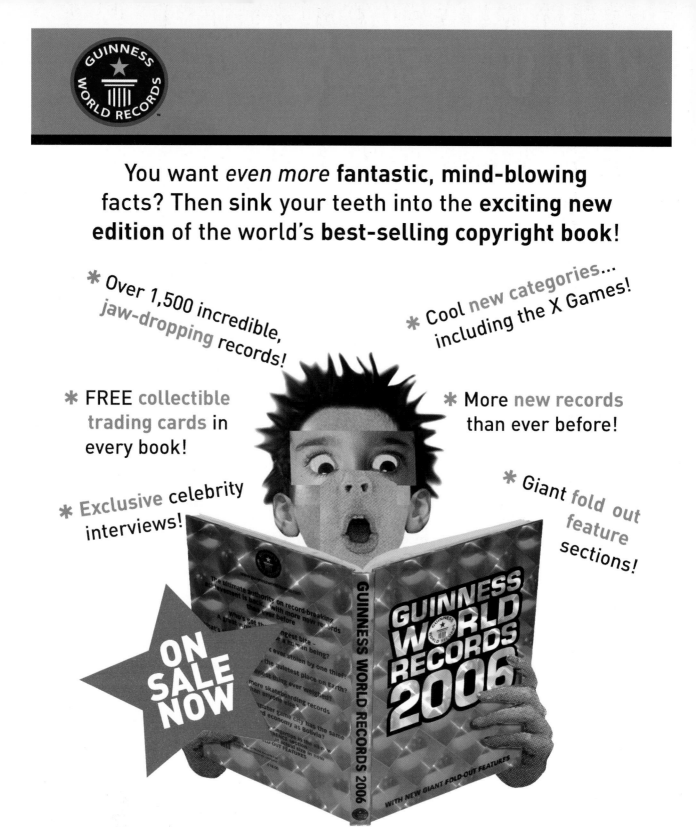